CALAMITY GOSPEL

Kyle Vaughn

Cover design based on an image created by the author.

ISBN: 9798375360294

Cerasus Poetry

London N22 6LY

cerasuspoetry.com

Thank you to:

My wife, Natalie, and my children, Eli, Charlotte, and Runa.

Robert Cochran and Alexander Etheridge, my poetry brothers.

Jack Myers, my poetry mentor.

CONTENTS

Psalm

In the after-light,
press me until I'm tiny

as a flea
on the wool of the lamb.

And when I am
lightning,
let me fall

inside the voice
rushing from the storm.

I

The Age of Infatuation

Believe Me

When does the onslaught of gladness begin?
A hundred thousand joys bob in
an ocean ready to be caught.

But I was always a poor swimmer,
turning green with the slightest wave,
choking on the water in a paper cup.

So imagine moving to
a rainless horizon and hoping
for spring to suddenly appear.

Every season's yield is desire
to place my skull beside me, to
remove my face with violence.

Or to sleep all night in
the presence of another, one
who is miraculously kind.

And don't you believe that if I could,
I would raise up a mountain
instead of the word or another silence?

Instead of this match head burning, a sun?
Would fill my body with love and blood.
I would be someone as beautiful as the wolf.

Someone with both halves of my face.
Someone that begins in green
and ends in blue stars.

This life insisted I memorize
the taste of heartache's wild
and remote beehive.

Too far to walk back with
anything sweet, anything to offer.
Lord, I just want to give myself away.

Honestly

Inside of me is this little bird
who rides a bicycle.

And when I see you,
my brain sends him a message to pedal faster.

Then we might catch up
enough to arrive at your face.

At Age 12

I didn't like wind pointing out my sad hairdo.
I had already begun to lose the battle with my body.

My army men spun on the wheel of reincarnation,
firecracked in the tunnels I dug in our suburban yard.

But I hid them behind my back
when neighbor kids rode bikes by.

At the skating rink, I ripped my pants right down the seam
in front of two girls with perfect skin and hair.

I passively hoped the DJ would save me.
Imagine my disappointment.

People really laughed that I should have washed more often.
Undressing tortured me and water seemed too endless.

I wasn't ready to be seated with others.
But I waited for amazement to come from outside.

Message for Deep Space

I waited for the school bus,
wrote a love note on the back of a math test.

The sum of x is your lemonade laugh,
all points on the graph, your irises.

I am an unstable particle, a tangram
of peanut butter sandwich triangles.

I am not the first atom, nor the last.
But everything that exists orbits my desire to kiss you.

The universe is expanding,
and you are my event horizon.

Communion

That name trembles like a bell.
What it was to be young and
meet someone. Knowing them

was an attempt at forever, however
impermanent. Every voice
was alive, every bottle, a bottle

of wine. Evening in the yard,
a forge in which to learn
to turn language into a kiss.

Kindergarten

Always I fell to the ground or scraped
a knee or traded lunch for something sweet.

Buried an apple to see if it would grow.
Probably missing a tooth, my tongue

looking for its doorway. I wanted something
like wings, though didn't know what to call them.

Something to bend light and wind, to deflect
the battering ram of a deep voice. I learned the primary colors,

and the secondary ones, put leaves of their kind in my pocket.
Like gold from some proverb my grandmother loved.

Something she said was necessary for the vegetable
and animal world. Something with earth. But I never

learned the secret of seeds. I learned how clay pots
ruin in the rain. And of course I demolished things—

classmates' piles of stones, sugarcube castles.
Scissored the head off a cutout farmer and blamed

a mythological creature. There was nowhere the devil's
rumble could be kept. My daydream went something like this:

my veins emptying into sleep, my body floating beyond myself.
My nightmare like this: failing to be deaf to anger—the quakes

that disarranged the house. But I opened the brass door of
a girl's hair, learned to disappear through her and

into a horizon. Learned to make a face and fly.
I cut two holes in a box to be a gold droid.

Made a spacecraft out of thin air. First day of a journey
beyond this weird planet. I wouldn't be cold out toward stars,

her eyes an antidote to deep space, her love note
pinned to my jacket like the flag of my homeland.

Sotto Voce

Let me introduce you to little me,
waiting for someone to hold my hand
to cross the road. But I never asked
for help, fearing what my voice
would summon. I went on with
insufferable wordlessness. With a straight
face. Made my action figures weep instead.
Banished them to a pit or dropped them
from dark's pinnacle. I gave them names

or when it came time to read at night,
learned the names of everything else—
timberwolf, weirkeeper, Vega, colophon.
Read the dictionary in my head.
I learned the words I can't say because
your eyes. When I was a child, I was
exposed to rain. Water—clear, bright,
flawless—ascending the walls. I set
a boat out in it, putting faith in the craft
of a shipwright. But my own body listed,
took on waves, all while I thought about the soil.
Desire dropped its hand in like an oar, and met with
sandstone, bedrock. Sometimes, if I was lucky,
an agate or smoky quartz. Stones don't pronounce
your name. And just looking at a hillside or slag pile
or peak or anticline doesn't translate to my asking.

I've never learned to ask for what I need. But what is it
that no one stops at the curb, reaches down, and takes me?

Calamity Gospel

I lived a weatherbeaten childhood on the plains.
One always had to read the color of the sky.
The signs of the spirit came only with a green afternoon,

prayers more urgent with the failure of the cloud.
Some angel laid waste to ten city blocks with
only a stare. Crumpled the grain elevator and

stripped a thousand mesquite trees clean.
In those fields, weeds rise night after night under
a poison moon. It darkblazes a way.

Once that moon fell into a rubbish heap, and
my only light was a television glow.
My hands held up a flickering blue and

couldn't cover over my unfixed faces anymore.
So I carved new eyes to see by clocklight,
to feel the way to long sleep.

On the plains, sunset is an opiate window,
the last apostasy before God blows you away.
But who am I to say what's holy or idol, one who

worshiped creation as beginning and end.
Believe me when I say a whipping came to pass
every time I looked at her too long.

God fixed on me with the bullet hole of His eye,
Harbormaster who sets my raft in firewhirls.
I heard of a spirit holy as dragonflies over mineral springs,

but for me that water was a long drink of cement.
And the ghost won't leave a message in something so stone,
nor in bones that recant their form.

So still I'm waiting on morning to raise its lantern like an altar.
Still my desire is for a body more than a funeral in waiting,
more than a gesture of a fruitless world meant to end.

More than a life lived in fear of the storm siren.
There is a world where I have a beautiful face,
one meant for love and news that is good.

Ministry

Have you seen in dead light
last crops and lonely disappearances?

The earth gives us grief as if
that were its only point.

Some fall blind in the road,
become better people.

But I have always thought the worst—
a murder on the way to Bible study.

No, I never followed those with the mark of Cain,
those kids in Arkansas who burned boxes in their yard.

But I've wanted to end myself more than once,
lay down in the corn rows with a shot to the head.

The only other feeling was that dark ministry to my body,
that libertine fever for anyone I saw.

How to get rid of that relic of desire?
I threw plenty of things in the bonfire.

Liquor bottles, matchbooks, telephone
numbers—all those things that turned my heart black.

Even left my knife at home
when I went out rambling at night.

I sunk love letters from the side of the boat,
a hurt animal floating on Lake Catherine.

But what good is purging if your heart isn't in it?
Ignorant whims have kept me in exile.

Driving back from the woods in a beat-up car,
I remembered lions ate people for real:

the servants of Christ, the simple people He loves.
I have tried to be one, but got mixed up what was the blood and
the word.

Living by the spirit is a walk without the body,
a devotion to evening's purple lanes.

I believe in holy fire, in horsemen, in hills made of skulls.
And I believe in thieves and the infirm. I am, after all.

Imagine being so ugly they dressed you as a corpse.
I've tried other outfits, bandaged my face, headed downtown.

But all my efforts to meet her eyes end with
a vanishing back into the casket of my room.

Anyway, the pool hall in Little Rock is closed now. †
Everyone says just go drink in the pines.

They act like they don't know the result of wood, gas, and matches,
stand on a ship bound for hell to spite it all.

Still, I keep a blank book for future confessions,
a place to sketch the shape of my thirst.

So forgive me again, repeat those wounds.
Minister to my need to be saved by savage blows.

†*This line after Frank Stanford*

"Down in the country, it almost make you cry"

—Charley Patton

I said her smile was an ivory bird from
the mouth's garden, but she made a sound
like winter and went deeper in the pines, a path

trimmed to the onset of early dark.
I could just make out some shapes, mostly
the sound of silver, like her eyes turned to river.

Like slow water, an old prophetic medium, like
children who walk blind to teach the body
its obligations. Even with the world in tears,

just look at God with His starburst heart of leaves.
Dry branches won't bend to make a crown and
heaven isn't a reflection of an ancient mountain.

I'm the fool following the last dust of ore
shook loose by a quake a hundred thousand
years after the fact. Broke as I could be,

Delta luck, a drink of the cheap stuff, money
a mockery. I began to look like a drowning.
You can believe I went without supper.

Going down the country, finding my head
in the mouth of the Gulf's oven. Finding
the temptation of a railroad bridge.

Floodwaters, Brazos River

Witness the dog-bit cloud's rampage.
What you had read in an old book is as far
away as you have ever known, as dull as

a forest beset with pine beetles.
Prayer became a little man
shouting into an uninhabited hatch.

A voice following a poor crow along the waterline.
By the time it reached an ear,
nobody was above ground.

Nobody dressed in nothing but
water, held in nothing but God's
agitated hand, beginning and end.

Taking Trash Out by Moonlight

Bearing this shape
to the garbage, trailing
ambient blood from meat

through a tear at the bottom—
the trash and I tunnel through
night-shafts: the dark's sack

of moons. When I hear
grinding glass under
sneakers, the clang of

a chain-linked perimeter, I am
not afraid of violence or even being
mistaken for a thief (though

I obsess over wounds I don't have).
I'm afraid of not being
human, not being able

to sit in the dining room chairs or to be
a part of interiors. I tread on
oblique shadows as if I won't

splinter them. I withdraw my belly
into my chest cavity, bloat the chambers
of my heart—but praise be this fat,

this blood, these lips drawn wordless
by experience: a silent toss of
waste into a hulking bin.

Poem on a Styrofoam Cup

All I saw on the way to work today:
brake lights, donut shops, and a purple
gorilla that sells Oldsmobiles.
I wanted a vision: something like

the burning sacred heart wrapped in
thorns, winging from my center.
When my ribs yawned open,
I birthed nothing more than newspapers

and packing peanuts. It was the office's
fault, of course. They didn't just want me
to work, they wanted me to believe.
So I exacted my revenge in stolen supplies

and secret notes slipped under the doors
of my coworkers: strange poems with
question-marks for titles and terrifyingly
ambiguous endings. I paid myself with time

in the shape of a daydream of her finger at
her lips, of being an image in her mind,
of bringing her a coffee and a book
and a walk in just the right light outside.

Making Myself Presentable

Early mornings, I carry the fat suit to toilet and water.
Make a disguise out of tiny typed lines.
Pretend my fingers in a circle are glasses.

The way to work is a tall crack of iron,
a street in the shape of a skull.
I grin to the bone.

I summit the staircase at the office, offer praise,
but really I want carts of limes—in rain—
in narrow mountain passes.

I want to find answers in ovens,
find that cardboard boxes are elaborate and lasting.
I want to be received in the city of my choosing.

For now, my opinion is solicited and at once ignored.
Though I wash and brush, my teeth rot, my beard grows wild,
a body apocalypse. I am beautiful and grossly out of control.

Naïve Melody

Concentrate, and you will find me
in the southerly folds of your map,

County Road 904. Think about my voice
long enough and your Triumph will

kickstart again, won't even need new tires,
will drive you where I'm crushed inside,

sorted into pieces—malfunctioned to obsolete—
so you can see this tapedeck where

I'm making you a mixtape.
Sounds of pedal steel, songs from the mud

and slow walks in oak groves.
There's nothing like the sound

of the early snow behind my face,
nothing as stunning as

your hair in stormfront wind.
Maybe my lyric amounts to nothing but

naïve melody, but I won't stop
the music or the delusion I can dance

as long as I'm between long nights
and the hope of your ink-dark yes.

The Age of Infatuation

At the carnival, features of her face loop in the rainbow light.
In the onset of evening her eyes appear the color of the nova.

I don't mind standing in line for the Ferris Wheel. I just want
to find her there looking into me.

If I came near enough, my lips would bloom, a flower would become
a boat, her shoulder a saltair coast. Near enough to touch her,

an art gallery would fill with whirlybirds and the professors
would have to leave her legs to live on in poetry. †

I desire to enter the poetry of the body
because I was made madeless.

I was made an idea and spoken,
left as an afterthought between a planet and its moon.

†*This line after Istvan Vas*

My desire for her eyes is an elliptical wilderness.
Over eons I come closer.

So imagine that quicksilvered kiss
when we turned the corner from the rest, tongues

sparking in an electric mandala,
a spinnaker gone off rails,

hurtling a thousand miles an hour
through our unfastened delight.

Her joy flames blonde rays all down the midway,
and I'm lit from the inside.

I reach for her hand, that little cloud,
the one holding our tickets for the ride.

Erase every era that is to come.
There won't be any greater time than this.

II

Tongue, Knife, Honey

Emanata

The best is your laugh like
70s grocery store music,

your belly of sunflowers,
gold and charcoal,

and the rainbow you made through
a light-leaking film camera.

The Human Being

This is the way to eternity: breath
cast in shapes of light: her mouth

exhaling a prayer: her arms
dressed in blue runes. Her body is

the nearest I come to
the testament in garnet script.

For proof, bodily proof, I need to hold
her savagery that is beyond decay.

I want to see limitless, want my eyes to swell like tide.
I need this world in order to save my body.

Calligraphed

"My lips and fingers were pens on her flesh:
I memorized her in every alphabet."
—Adonis

I want to write *binding* over your heart, to the left
of your breastbone, *center*, *delight*—in
cursive, illustrated with semicircles,
blue moons and waves. I want to drink

water from your hands, desire's river pressing
through my stone. Snow learned the channels of
my face, left me with icelit eyes that should have
seen more world. But I found the way in your

valleys. Let's say the map shows rapids
or boulders or the collision of tectonic plates. Where
do we go in an upended world? The answer is—
I'm gentle and have a navy made of words. I have

the language of another sunrise. So tell me
the Portuguese for *light*. Let me see the spark of a
mandarin in your mouth. Paint my face as it should
look and spell our names with your fingertips on my palms.

The Age

More bodies on the evening news.
Another knock-out at the party.

What was her name?
I drunk lazy quiet at the end of her eyes.

Help me to my car. I'll sleep there tonight.
No one's expecting me.

I'll worry in the morning about
my place among the masses.

I am breathtaken at slurred stars
hovering over millions of miles of smoke.

Drunk's Alchemy

Are you impressed
that I retrieved these jewels from
the mineshaft for you,

carried bent light in a Solo cup,
and poured it into electric sockets
that turned the night places off?

Then let me be your wine.
Drink me all the way to
the last ruby drop.

Recitation

I recite to you the one that says
the owl opens his eyes all night to the moon†.

I show you the image of the sound of the pines,
draw a legend on the map of a thunderbolt.

When your form passed behind a diaphanous screen,
I lost my mind among a gust of moths.

The distance of your city is a terrible green absence.
I send the wine back and ask for your address.

On paper you held, an envelope, is your incarnate tongue.
I went inside its question, *what wisdom teaches separation?* †

And I finally found that word you were looking for:
just ask, and I'll add it to your vocabulary.

†*Kabir*

Demanding More Song from the Music

In my vocabulary, all words are questions.
So translate your mouth for me, because I already believe.

I forget my name and the name of my town,
but I recite your lashes to drink you as divine.

Others may have stone forms or voices alive like beer,
but I can draw ink from your eyes to write lines down your side.

I have a book on your ankle,
another for your unraveled sandal.

Don't make me collect more relics or etch stoic faces in wood grain.
Answer me with your palms, with terraformed lines of poems.

Dusk is laddering up the eastern wall, age incarnate on my face.
So drown me today in baptismal waves of your hair.

Love Song at Civil Dusk

I was the one. I carved
your name into the psalter.

Remember when we embraced in
the tyrant's bath when he wasn't looking?

We left naked waterprints
on white tile.

I won't sleep, *won't*, until
I stare your earthen eye into my book.

For you, I remain on stormwatch with
a dozen belted daggers.

I camp on the edge of an anesthetic forest.
One small spark and the whole thing catches blaze.

My Gift to the Metropolitan Museum of Art

When the museum guard wasn't looking, I added a little
something for you to that wedding portrait from the *Shahnama*.
Can you guess what it is?

I asked Hafez how I could arrive at your door.
He said he made the trip with
the help of the bird of Solomon.

But I can't tell a blackbird from a crow!
Was this a migratory bird
or a messenger pigeon?

I should have paid more attention in school,
but I was already dreaming
of your legs descending a staircase.

Until now, the sum of my achievements
was one carved verse
on the altar I tore from my side.

I received the word before the vision,
my love before your face,
my exile before my country.

But now all the lovers of art can enjoy
one bright rose
in the corner of the scene.

Psalm

I was born inside the folds of glass,
grew up in the furnace, live between
midnight breath and pine.

I flood and I thirst, I poison and quiet,
I flower and die. The mirror is my cipher
and doubt is my homeland.

You are fossils in my garden, I must
discover you. I am the epoch,
the dust that erodes itself.

Still, there is a psalm inside me,
a badland's windless terrain, that
begs for you all night through.

The Living Word

I write *tenderness*
on your heel, *paradise*
on your thigh.

In the space between your
shoulder blades, a vowel
pronounces your form.

I repeat your face
as a mantra,
memorize your eyes like

a calendar of moons.
Your image, your borderless body
fills a valley with snow.

Even only in my imagination,
you are a reminder of being
rather than nonbeing.

Still, I want what I shouldn't want,
like when your tongue
cleans the knife after honey.

Offer me a deep to taste,
a skyline to speak an evening to.
I want to see halos coronate us all night.

III

Deep Ellum

Diner Days

I sat in a booth, lifting and lowering a cup,
just to understand interiors reflected in a plate glass window.

First love, who let me for a while shelter,
I saw I was not the person you were looking for.

So I colored my insides with the shapes in an orange plastic bottle,
inked out wants like crows driven mad by gunfire.

I carved bigger eyes to find my way by clocklight.
Traveling in the dark seems forever.

Three decades pass, and I remember
the rightful look of cirrus above a stormswept field

and the sound of electropop in a pickup truck
and holding in my hand your bubblegum

which came from the machine
by the entrance of an all-night diner.

The Party

Pills from a briefcase multiplied stars.
Glass orbited my skull.

A girl loved me for bringing
flavored liquor from the beer store.

I was not afraid of the backlit eyes of the crow.
Someone released the skeleton of a dog to roam the empty
of where I lived.

The boy who was terminally ill
told me a white noise like nine thousand voices was trying
to kill him.

Plainclothes cops knocked on the door,
but we were gone.

Deep Ellum

It is the hour to find a corner,
concussive, with everything electric on.

The message says *Jewelry Guns Layaway.* I listen.
It is midnight in my gut, iron in my blood is crying.

Something is breathing up ahead in the gully weeds.
Women are loosening their collars.

I give it all away, use a fake name,
vomit a darkness misunderstood as nightshine.

For my beast, there is no jail, no drunk-tank cell.
Just needles in the street and cigarette ends in the bushes.

Whatever I hear is poisoned by the applause of falling wings
    that ruptured me.
But will peeling off my fingerprints liberate my name?

Debris is my signature, my fingertip
at temple, thumb cocked back.

In the alley, there is a monolith:
hateful box springs like a last corridor.

Go with me.
Go with me there.

Exhaust

Horn-blares, traffic-scattered exhaust, birds
migrating from lamppost to lamppost:

I check the train schedule, hope to find
a short wait, body to be moving soon,

passing along through tunnels and rail
crossings, thinking of her mouth, darkly

open after a question, and my inability
to say what's real: this street? this station?

these empty ears and nausea?
these cloudy passengers?—ghosts that

sprouted arms to pummel the dark,
thumbs to excavate the stone from a cherry.

God bellyaches over my doubt,
chokes me dry, threatens my blood.

Dares me enjoy the world,
taste the snowfall and trust the sickle and flame.

After all, why cast away the ephemeral?:
corn husks cluttered among my remembrances,

light trails of taillights, severed
telephone that disarranges our words.

Driving Down Live Oak, East Dallas

Rage-pinched faces sear into the street,
exiles from gutted buildings.

I belong here, swim through
cement on four drunk tires.

I can scream out loud, rattling
beer bottles and scattering trade papers.

A tangled bird looks at me with
an eye turned prism, an eye turned cherry.

Waving me over—a hungry
woman in umbrella shadow.

She's hiding drugs inside her.
The heat hunts her with teeth,

heaves into her blood,
leaves her body voided in weeds.

I, too, slump, pose over the steering wheel,
portrait of the sick with midnight crown.

The Unwashed Phenomenon

I lost my mind to boiling water,
gone soft in the mud of useless words.
By that time, I was a diagnosed wanderer
lost to the jaws of a dog and deep in debt.

I ate like you wouldn't believe: salted pork,
beef with hickory sauce, cola and cane sugar, river fries.
I drank with my eyes until everyone was stripped.
I made known what men want at night.

That's how dust meets its end in rain,
thinking to bare itself to find its helpmate.
But the Earth routs itself at the appointed time.
The body, too—cuts its own throat.

I was wrecked in the cold. The river never
froze enough to step off the bank.
Medication was a feat of lightning,
but an arc too brief to fix me.

Went down to visit the Sisters of Misery,
bought one of their quilts made from a widow's scraps.
That thing was sewed up with enough grief
you'd be crazy to look at it.

Months were just segments of the worm:
the poor gave birth and the drowned were lifted to the surface.
I became a child pressed to the ice of a bus window.
I shuddered in the canal.

Everything was appetite—not even
the taste of the wound of the apple could disrupt me.
Not even the hymnal worked
miming the light of *I'll Fly Away*.

Black wings are painful,
especially worn on boats sunk
en route to the country of imagination.
Night on the water was quiet, too quiet.

Even back home, the only sound is a packmule.
Branches grow on the ceiling and you wouldn't ever
know or find a way to explain.
But even the way granddad dries his hands has a meaning.

The story of the bird of Solomon was
the only one I ever really understood.
Sent out for the Lord's task, returned with saving grace,
and was punished anyway.

His brothers, those exiled birds in the mountains, are
species of the four parts of fire:
fuel, invisible, blueflame, and crest.
It's no wonder the smoke flies away.

I've heard tell of light everywhere,
emanata from the mouth of an ivory lamb.
But the best I can do is weep my heart out
at a knotty root shrine.

The secret of love is to be calm about punishment.
Think of it as the vacancy of a grave.
It'll be filled up soon enough
and rest assured you won't come back.

God's love is a sickle blow
wrapped in violence around my face.
I am an unwinding rootless vine set apart from its tree
on its thousand year journey to stone.

Many women were in that forest,
all with a bag of eyes in one hand and a hammer in the other.
When they finished with me,
they could think of nothing but blood.

Heed the Lord and let Him be in dark charge.
Better fear desires that make pears a raving shame.
Better dream of a myth's long mercy.
Whip your little heart, dry and puny.

Do you know what the preacher preaches?
A sermon alone in the bathroom,
a rumination on childhood as a nervous army
burning jungles and caving in faces with the stocks of guns.

The revival tent was no place to be. That summer was
a barnburner. You never knew what would go up next.
The attic, neighbor's car, the corner store.
The instant it catches, a hundred feet of smoke.

And how did I find myself in a camp with three convalescent
wards?
As they say, hospitals are for the ill.
I had buried the entrance to the cathouse, but not enough to
look away.
I piled newspapers in front of the door as if that was enough to
quit desire.

I came out of bed with long arms. I changed
my face with a knife, heard water in
the fish's belly, a coin on its eye,
Siva on the face of the coin.

I came out of bed with long arms
after drinking limewater at night,
a spirit moving in three-dimensional space,
a pair of lungs at the bottom of the lake.

I just about worked a gun to sprout lead in bone.
Held it to my temple and let out a yelp.
But thought of my dear mother and instead
let a man hold my head underwater.

If you are lost, you have arrived at my eyes,
arrived at a number of locks to shut against a mad country.
I am the addict who swallowed the poison,
strangled on the wafer from the very wounded hand.

I am low down. Sent out
for news of the apostates, only to find
my own guts on the ground.
I am marked with mulberries over my eyes.

Scattered with fruit unworthy of an offering,
I only look at the land over there.
I wander with the downstream people,
the unwashed among the unwashed.

Mania's Tyranny

I believe in bodies lit like an arcade, turned electric by a voltage real as bones. I strip down deep, undoing myself to straddle a blaze. That flame descended, then rose in fever, forging a hundred worthless ingots back into my head. Ask for fire and you get a forest turned to black rock. You get that angel with the glowing briquette pressed to your lips. He even tried to take my hands off. I hid them underneath a lady's red coat. My lust could break a river in two. And turn water to smoke, every last curl for my lungs. Especially if it's fatal. Especially if it singes like the upholstery burn where the cherry fell out. Especially if it is the planet of her body, any body. Watch me chain myself to her waist. Watch me call wind from a barren field, unchain a fat green sky. Crown myself with rain and turn the blur of my speed into a bloodhungry lion. I give my teeth to your arm. I give out gold, a drunk's alchemy. I give yellow to every shadow. The only light is my body, and my bones are a path, an ordeal all night inside a furnace. Smoke's overflow—maniac arms of black unravel, holding out spirits to taste every heaven, holding out eggs of the earth, monuments of faces, and the savage jaws of animals. And inside all of this is an open throat, a casket full of something dynamic, thunderheads of birds mushrooming in every direction—ten thousand melted glass hummingbirds. I am everywhere, digging scrap-iron from the guts of the earth, erecting a tinfoil monument to my imaginary friends. And collecting things: seaglass, ticket-stubs, empty root beer bottles. Green army men, breakups, coins with holes in them. Xerographed poems, atlases, stamps with holy iconography. Unholy and insincere prayers. Ugliness and sleeplessness. Swear words, door slams, and declarations of love. I carve everything into an altar, a feast of tabernacles, and a thousand years of stained glass. I learn to burn in my cell. I always learn the hard way: immolated, sunburst, firebird, revival.

Depression's Exile

My dread fell halfway through the stars. Green shadows
made me wonder about the kingdom of heaven. My song
didn't seem to fit beneath the tree. Schoolchildren's subtraction

left me with less than I could use to float on. Minus two barrels.
Minus two arms for oars. Ahead I saw the branches of the river
and on each bank, a child of Adam. They held pictures

of their ancestor—no, just quarks from some forsaken genesis.
I created only trouble in the cemetery, waving my undershirt like
a surrender, riding a black horse up and down the aisles.

Grief as Compass

The expanse of sky is not a direction.
But you set off anyway, like you could navigate
the country on foot. You unraveled

your best sentences from the fire, typed them
on raw paper, folded, folded, and let fly
at low altitude. The Earth is still perfect.

Your child's mouth no longer exists. You saved
his teeth in an envelope in a drawer. Blood means
everything. Blood was a lamp.

You wanted the company of a loved one.
The light couldn't be bothered
to show him the way.

Tranquility Base

The name is so close.
But missing its loneliness.

Stone affixed to the horizon—
sometimes a key, sometimes a blade.

And I have gone as silent as
the moon's white ice of time.

Her face ascended so what good
are words, what else is necessary?

I am only as near as a footprint in
minerals, an earthshadow in evening.

Slanted light is the world's incomparable
obstacle—the wind that follows the wind.

The solitude that follows my love—folded
into a message sent to another world.

Grief as Nocturne

Dear world, page whose loneliness
I read like a picture book and set down

like cursed gospel with red penciled in every *o*.
The end's glow worn as a post-meridian crown.

It is night's incline. A last walk through columbine
and black chokeberry that put an end to my eyes.

What does it matter if I sleep another hour?
Light is punctuated, weather dead as ancestors.

Dead as writing, the bend of every letter
born out of crushed white bone.

For KS, Wichita Falls State Hospital

It was hard to make out your words
from the pay telephone of the ward,
hard to tell what was true:

You said your insides were sculpted by bees and
that though you pushed harder on the crown of thorns,
you didn't know why you had to be there.

Cigarette burns tree-ringed your arms.
I looked in the door behind your little hands and
found a pile of stolen clothes.

Silver keys spilled from a dollhouse door
behind which you kept love pictures in crayon
and a dead twin.

I'd never seen such transformation, your eyes
looking out from three flattened faces.
I would have carried you home if that would have saved you.

Suicide and Survivor

for RA and JA

Hands are beautiful as boats
ferrying the dead away

and returning the living
to a deserted beachhead.

This or that seems a miracle, but water
more water forces us into a mirror

and the bottom disappears.
Nothing we do rises.

The way we float becomes
heavier, salt even heavier.

The survivors from some outrage,
from some mangled time,

continue in a manner beyond our ability.
Kneel and kneel more,

pressing into the Wounds
to remember the body is a body.

Carry that last fire into a dry season.
The forest opens

to dark purple wind.
Bones hurt. The word

comes free. Please, you,
Lord, Father, anything.

We need to know.
Was there an origin before suffering?

Is there a branch, a sprig to catch hold?
The other world begins with

water, light, clear.
Dayrise. Unburial.

Dear child, you fell in acute loss,
grief's rubble snowing into the way.

In memoriam, here are my arms,
making a shape that means *safe*.

Anti-Sermon: Mania

I was born human, no heart but this one, no
eyes, no eyes but these lamed by fire,

blazing through crowds with teenaged
hunger, coughing at the memory

of Lucky Strikes. I am known
at the edge of town: junkpile with

carparts, discarded stoves fringed by grass,
rickety light from aluminum,

and dogs, their boiled voices
barking at street music.

I don't want to be good, but a creature,
haunted silver thing clutching

the mountain, tearing out roots and
gemstones purple as air.

If you are a stranger, show me your
irises, how they are both

bright and black. Wash me in
rainwater, ruined by smokestacks.

Erase me with the heaven of abandoned buildings,
high empty animals crowned by midnight.

Her Name as Lightning

It was too late in the age
to be pining for the sky's white

branch in the distance. It was time
to invent that light, a fire that

made a drink into a child's voice,
a drink of fog from the old woods.

A walk with her in the lodgepoles and cedars.
Heaven's promise is a waving off of nightmares.

I thought I'd find answers in the midnight
wilderness of her hair. But the world is adjacent

to hell. And her address is now on a far coast,
its numbers as invisible as God's answer to

the pains of time. The blame—everywhere—
from a pile of empty shoes to a minefield

of smoked cigarettes. I needed her word. Needed
a compass for her direction. Every cellblock on

the calendar erupted. Every morning, buckshot, and
every day's answer, a burst of hawk feathers.

I only knew her name, but Lord, I wanted to taste
her lips to amend the second hand. To understand

the panther's stillness. To hear between the notes of the
tanager. To find a silence as familiar as birth.

Inscape with Aviary

I have heard the myna speak nonsense,
his chatter like laughter amounting to nothing but trouble at home.

His throat's interior, a mystery—and mine:
essentially body-less, razor-like ideations.

He is only knowable
after turquoise rupture.

The mystery is poison
and how I kept on after ingesting.

Hunger nearly ended the one
who tried everything as food.

It was the blueberries,
sad buckshot of blueberries,

round as the eggs of an invasive species,
a crazy bird among them, heckling anyone near.

In the center of my belly,
I placed the Sinaloa crow,

the one wearing black
as the image of a martyr.

He insisted on nesting
in a tree of thorns.

Forgive me who is between comfort
and the seven cords of the scourge.

On the one hand, I'm untangling
miles of spilled insides.

The other, I'm setting out fruit
for that flock of released pet parakeets.

Their color is for me,
but my blood makes a threatening noise.

A miracle would be
the return of the owl.

Saw him that once
in my nights behind glass.

But best of all would be
an olive ibis in mangroves.

That one's outside of me
guarding his boat tied to the roots.

Lonely child, I made a bird
out of driftwood and twine.

I still believe he'll fly
into a cloud that won't rain away.

Untranslatable

Another gleaming fall rises like glass to
contain another solitude, a bird
following its music into a rhythm against a window,
knocking against invisible limits. Injury can't

be helped by night's insufferable gauze.
And where is the entrance to the convalescent ward?
Where is the market for antidotes for a poisoned voice?
Someone holy gives me a word I won't listen to, one

I'll hide in a childhood memory of a lost balloon.
I am not who I was. I amputated that boy, left his
limbs to the jaws of a masterless dog.
Learned the artfulness of my own incisors. Bloody mouth,

I could only drink smoke from a porcelain cup, and
my name diminished into a wordless fool.
Found other ways to leave messages, writing
letters in big black script. With a green beer bottle,

I imitated the poem of the drunk,
emerald lines with lost hope about bones.
And there again, silence's circumference.
What can be said about a lifetime of grief? I cannot

explain the way through disaster, but
I know the look and the meaning of the shore.
It's why I return to the image of a face, something that's
divine and quiet and not an edge to collide with.

IV

Forgive Me

Volta: Late Prayer

Are you one that can believe good news?
Some say their body will never die. Myself,

I ate strychnine from a pretty red wrapper today.
I am a terrible person with an identity

of desire. With one love,
I was a fool. To another, a thug.

Performed naive stunts in
an arrogant cruciform pose.

The world's every slaughter and
madness was born in me.

I have waited on regret's green road,
wasting moments I could have knelt.

See the way of trouble's path through the color
of my hair. Inter last hope in an elegiac form.

I have already been hushed in
a long, nameless burial.

What I desire most has no name but *end*.
I repeat it with a mouth of unbound smoke.

Save me from a path of coals. Free me
from her neon eyes.

Yes, I've kept vigil at an unholy gate, risked
my throat for her shape, nearly

harvested all the straw of my life with
the sickle blow of God's love. What a privilege

to carry my Savior to wood and nails. Imagine
what it's like to be my true love. I have tried

to wash in the fountain, but can't keep
two drops steady in my palms.

When the tremors started, I knew it was
my sentence. Still, I believe—

like every day's miracle—
hands, resurrection, a turning, endless end.

All, Rise

The old world was on fire, its round
hunger darkening, its night
disappearing into thundershower.

I had taken my bike down to the rest home,
its old tires slouching along the macadam.
Walked it through the cemetery, as one ought.

Grandad couldn't speak by then. Acted like
he seen a holy being, maybe even
the ghosts of my two dead girls.

But I knew enough to know what he'd say,
spirits or not. He'd frame it all with some calamity—
a man lost in the logging fields, baby sister

down with the cancer. Or his favorite story, the quail
on the icy lake that starving winter. The one we wanted
to hear was about the boar that nearly tore his guts out in

the woods behind Trout-Goodpine High School. Or
we liked just to sit in his quiet, watch him watch nothing
in particular. Watch him study the treeline like it was alive.

His clothes smelled like eucalyptus leaves, which always
made it seem he had stepped through some door that never was.
That land was green and sideways enough to hide just out of view.

This land is wrong. A buried town beyond the horizon isn't
a hope we can hold. The older you get, the less the way seems
passable in any season. Ice begets ice in a childhood tale,

white scent like the space between a lake and the wood.
But stories die a little each godforsaken year, and the newspaper
says every tree on the windward side is now just ash.

Imagine what it means if just one survives. That's something
    to hold,
a thing beyond things. A life beyond time. Lightning is a measure
of breath, a secondhand rounding the foot of the clock. Not even

Christ can look away from the horse's silent path.
Autumn burns with its own discovery—
man's eyes as brittle as mothwings,

fear buried like a yellow diamond.
Fear of the end rising like the congregation
for the reading of God's word. Old age calling out

like the rasp of black lungs.
Feel it take shape like a hole in the ground.
Feel it like the last stair in the dark.

If, after everything, you're remade,
your voice will be an element set on
a table like bread. The kind eaten
as part of miracle. We are here as elements

and miracles. Transfiguration.
A mirror becomes an animal,
something living to see us and
not forget. We're to learn to bend

a question into a blank. Make
today's imaginary kingdom into
a child's eyes. Raise a field, wild,
into a blackoak grove. And yet

roots find their errors. Impassable mass.
Dust's habitat in the lung.
An atom becomes cancer,
September becomes a tomb.

My mind becomes a kind of poison.
My thumb and finger,
hammer and barrel of a gun.
My book sunk in an old pond.

Water melted my insides,
slaked lime, remarkable damage.
Water becomes a calendar,
its endless grid a punishing city,

its endless shed held in a single drop.
You drown in ritual, rattle as
time's skeleton. But if you can explain
the land as light and light as amber

and amber with a word,
you have birthed a name
where there is no name
You have made bracken into paradise.

Augustine Variation

Some lives are made for ruby-hearted booze
out in some dancehall that might mean joy.

Writing meant a sacrament in remembrance of bees,
every dead heart stacked neat like a hive.

My word is a lamb that confessed so to be drowned.
Don't bother interrogate it over crushed blackberry bushes.

Even the river says it doesn't matter,
flowing into a narrative now ten sleeps deep.

Some lives are the spill of wine in a white room,
arms of another thirst forming a transept.

My words taste the way salt sounds,
like a rainy month consuming a hill.

Like the smile of an effigy
as it burns to the ground.

Servant of the Lord, Look at the Clod

Before dying
you must understand the magic needed
to get through water.
Walk the past to a coast
to a letter you wrote someone
who you know is
lonely twenty years after the fact:
a good person
with the clearest heart of them all.
Amen.

Write another letter past summer snow,
that far north:
the details of a ghost,
of God pinning your bones like
a moth to certain positions.
Don't leave out the part
about hiding under waves with small gills
or calling
fruitlessly to someone
you watched go too far from shore.

Don't leave out the boy
with brittle bone disease,
his parents who loved him with
a newsprint quiet.
But you can imply that professor,
the rheumatic polymath,
and skip over the list of
every death in a Victorian novel.

Sign it *Your Future Self* or
Your Terror.
Post it in sick white halls
in remembrance of
empty spaces
willfully carved from the dead.

Black Song to Open a Window

Wind opened a path through trees,
a distance of ash.

Green borders darken in rain.
The high, angry gates of thunderheads, unmerciful.

Now let us praise Him.
Now, the saying goes.

*

August approaches. Sleep is a greenhouse.
The need for emotional words is water.
These are the words: master, teacher, servant, child.
And now a dark sun is lower, even lower.

*

The humiliation of the body,
the distance from infant to infirmed
painted white as a hospital—
make us afraid,
make us.

*

And now a word's orchard—
rain's glass fills a narrow corridor,
reflecting faces as endless as a Janus mask.
Anything made can be unmade.

*

Nothing can match the hatred of a son.
The star is nothing to the night.

*

Eyes silent as a dictionary.
Dust and ash are wordless.

*

Poor heart, food for birds,
shut out of the gates of mercy.
It darkens, finds itself
the opposite of a wind.
The earth and its beings
stay and go, open and close,
easily overcome.

*

The Lord loveth the gates of Too-Dark.
To live is to be oppressed by heat,
to be hungry, to eat, and be hungry again.
Sorrow is in a pot, in a well.
But these gates go all the way through
to the loveliest place.
The windows open
on a ground of sun-green stones.

Triumphal Entry of One Who Survived Himself

"...over him: a mighty stone. Always longing to cast it away from his head, he wanders far from the joy of festivity."
—Pindar

In all our end rites—pyre,
handful of earth, entrance on donkey—
do any call for air?

I wrote your name there.
According to the principles of art,
this means you may pass.

Death, like theft, may ask *where are your eyes?*
only because you knew the way by heart.
You just wanted to burn,

become color in a portrait of the Gauls.
Strange is that work to disrupt
the necessary things in life.

Pray at the edge between language and a stone.
Make a stroke in the style of the old masters.
It's not enough just to think of the sun.

Arms unfolded, take in the season for a while.
And stay in it, stay
in a long slaughter of flames.

Photo, Age 18

Bluegreen bird, desire as notes of
a song with pedal steel, lemon

air all swallowed up in
a sky. My hair is a wave, high

tide. Tan chest. Necklace from a girl.
All my teeth. The person here is silent,

unable to look beyond July. Under
my eyes, the glint of a blade.

I thought myself horrid.
But if I knew—if I—what I

wouldn't give to be
more kind to myself.

If I had been more able, surely
I would have spared myself one ray.

Forgive Me

The first day of third grade, I stood up and announced
I wanted to cut my heart out with the buck knife I got on
summer vacation.

There are two things I'm good at: losing and making a scene,
so when it came to my pride, I said *why the hell not.*

And by this age, I thought carnage was normal.
I delivered this news as a matter of fact.

That fact of harm repeated in my skull
through years of birdshot fantasy.

For me to stop imagining in an endless loop my brains blown out,
there had to be love to meditate on.

I found love's image, I think,
though, mostly alone, I must often be its silent mirror.

Still, some nights I have to crawl in dust to put my guts back in,
so forgive me when I enjoy a Coke or marvel at a tiny toy airplane.

Better yet, forgive me for finding the divine in the midnight joy of
    your body,
or joy in the body of the divine, when I can manage that belief.

To my report, my teacher only said *oh, ok*.
She didn't know the first thing about suffering.

Ten years later, another boy in that class
would open a hole in his chest because a girl didn't love him.

Thank God I didn't do it.
Though I could have and could still.

But now I get to see my daughter push back the hair from her face
and see the dance in her bones

and this, more beautiful, because I am so awful,
yet mercy mercy so alive.

From Love's Monolith to the End

I let her rest on my arm while
Blood on the Tracks spun to the end.

That moment may have proven I was
human—tender, wild, and good.

After sleeping, I woke to find her eyes
opening like a cigarette case with noon inside.

We drove west to Abilene to find
a clearer view of thunderheads.

In my favorite photo, you're in the road,
your Leica trained on me.

Lighter in your black jacket, tobacco, and papers.
The span of your shoulders magnifies even these last years.

You will be that age forever, with an eye for the
beauty of a rusted engine, the sense of a storm's destination.

Like that day's approaching bow echo,
the atmosphere of your face,

the rebel love you bore
placed your likeness ever in who I am.

Restoration

Ten years later, I swear she's still coming toward me
through the tall grass, in boots, holding a pinhole camera,

all my powers inflated
and released, balloon-shaped, into sky.

Memory is a boundless visitation,
unburying our eyes:

a hornet that threads consciousness
among the leaves of high branches.

It interrupts our view of storm:
arms of hurricane doubling back, few clear moments,

though even now, her hidden cigarettes
are burning in an unlit room, her face limned by the glow.

Fountain

I went to school here.
Learned to smoke there
where a fountain once was.

Learned about Einstein's lies.
Now I know I can't go back
to tracing your waistline.

I revisit the library
from which you drunkenly
fell a story and survived.

The end of life is storming the air
just behind my body,
not wholly unlike when I rushed

into eighteen and nearly poisoned myself.
Still, still, I've never seen a face like yours
so glad to greet me after Astronomy.

I remember in pecan groves the intersection
of your arms and hips,
how you gathered fall.

We played that song that was
the color of cherries
in the parking lot of the Thunderbird Motel.

I know I can't return to that possibility
of bodies in joy, but no one can touch
our afternoons with records, tea, and smokes.

Genesis

I have cycled through the numbers
on the face of a severe clock.

With fountainous sounds,
you named for me the states of laughter, sleep, and birth.

I have seen a miracle,
a genesis folded as light that spins,

once around
for every good year.

Airmail

I want to thank that letter-carrier in Kenya
who bore our words as bottomless diamonds in his rucksack,

who left them as wild birds
nesting in mailboxes.

The Human Condition

Witness life's drift to winter
solstice twilight: afternoon falls
on the open book, hatching it
into unbearable variations of light,

day's golden clock halting into
sudden onset of dark, and then
night reflecting in the river its
grove of silver-faced moons.

The sky grows little. A gust
swallows the fissured glass of my heart.
To learn it will all go—the people,
my loves. Once there was proof of

life—your infant foot in my palm.
And then wind's signal to the diaspora
of my younger selves. I grew old
on a long walk, December's spike of

woodsmoke in my throat. You grew
little again, suffering's ordination,
unbearable variations of grief's mask.
Every last atom of me is a prayer:

pick up thy bed and walk.
Though there is black water,
come into the shoals. Come,
if you must, on your knees,

to mercy's ascent, the dark rising to
a star's precision. In holy light's
calculations, all arrives at the moment,
the right moment for our salvation.

Walk

Ascended into forest dusk
to quarry a slowburst memory
before my early death.

Found an animal's burrow,
a black and blue feather,
and starry minerals.

My daughter studied deep red berries,
advised that one never knew
whether they were poison or power.

Autobiography of a Storm

That year, things refused to speak
other than laughter in the dark.
Ferrous sky not unlike the purple bruise I was
at birth. I was blood's spark surrounded by a dry forest.
Hollowed by God's sanguine weapon of others.
Everywhere was wilderness.
Everywhere was sacrifice, crowns of knives in animal skulls.
What is pain but a mirror made of bone?

Two hemispheres of the mind—one, an arbor—
the other, an aperture. A garnet eye looking back
through unforgiving disfigurement. Lightning was
a ghost finding its way to water, a starry instrument
falling from the doctor's bag. It cracked, another
heart struck on the anvil. Story of how the elm
burned from the inside. And the house, also inseparable
from its fire. Doorways, burning. Windowless desolation,
burning.

Story of any old calamity—outbreak of yellow fever,
consumption, roadway accident. Infants' graves and
a whole doctrine of coffins. Think of the simple image of
night's return through the conifers—sackcloth, ashes. And
no one remembers if the Savior bore a word for me like a rusted
fishmonger, an execution hanging from his neck. And his
grievous eyes. His silver face pressed like a cloud to the
beginnings of the land. An assault of light to give us clear air.

Appendix

I have finished the song. Firelight
is my mind. Night becomes a blunted

mountain. The plain fills with vines
of wind, the world's mercy reduced

to a darkgreen winnow. In a thunderbolt,
I saw the shadow's way vanish

into the black of the animals' mouths.
Praise all things, praise.

Blessings from the moorhen,
the roan. And changelings—beings

set upright to go out beyond our lives.
Walking to the morning of the other world.

Notes

"Down in the country, it almost make you cry": The title of this poem is a lyric from Charley Patton's "'34 Blues"

"Love Song at Civil Dusk" is for Natalie

"Psalm" ("I was born inside the folds of glass...") is after Adonis

"The Unwashed Phenomenon" is after Frank Stanford and the title is a lyric from Joan Baez's "Diamonds and Rust"

"Genesis" is for Charlotte

"Airmail" is for Natalie

"The Human Condition" is for Eli

"Walk" is for Charlotte and Runa

Appendix

Thank you to the editors of the following journals and anthologies in which these poems, sometimes in earlier versions, first appeared:

"Raised to Walk in Newness of Life" in *The Journal*

"All, Rise" and "Down in the country, it almost make you cry" in the museum of americana

"Photo, Age 18" and "Recitation" in Marías at Sampaguitas

"Ministry" in *Juke Joint*

"Kindergarten" and "Depression's Exile" in *Tír na nÓg*

"Calligraphed" in *A-Minor*

"Untranslatable" in *Emerge Literary Journal*

"Augustine Variation" in *Dawntreader*

"Triumphal Entry of One Who Survived Himself" in *Abridged*

"Grief as Compass" (formerly "Memory of September") and "Inscape with Aviary" in *The Shore*

"Fountain" and "From Love's Monolith to the End" in *Orange Blush Zine*

"Naïve Melody" in *The Boiler*

"The Party" and "At Age Twelve" in *Vinyl Poetry and Prose*

"Exhaust" in *Drunken Boat*

"Taking Trash Out by Moonlight" in *Disembodied Text*

"Poem on a Styrofoam Cup" and "Honestly" in *BlazeVOX*

"Genesis" (formerly "Letter to My Imagined Daughter") in *The Sentence*, *Introduction to the Prose Poem* (Firewheel Editions), and *Prose Poetry: An Introduction* (Princeton UP)

About the Author

Kyle Vaughn is the author of the poetry chapbook *The Alpinist Searches Lonely Places* (Belle Point Press, 2022), *Lightning Paths: 75 Poetry Writing Exercises* (NCTE Books, 2018), and is the co-author/co-photographer of *A New Light in Kalighat* (American Councils for International Education, 2013).

His poems have appeared in journals such as *The Journal*, *A-Minor*, *The Boiler*, *Drunken Boat*, *Poetry East*, *Vinyl*, *the museum of americana* (2022 Best of the Net nomination), and *The Shore* (2021 Pushcart Prize nomination).

His prose has appeared in *English Journal*, and his photography in *Annalemma* and *Holon*.

Find him at www.kylevaughn.org.

www.ingramcontent.com/pod-product-compliance
Lightning Source LLC
LaVergne TN
LVHW010117170826
845678LV00012B/2445

* 9 7 9 8 3 7 5 3 6 0 2 9 4 *